Photocopiable

The Positive Behaviour Book

75 Practical Strategies for Managing Classroom Behaviours

Patricia Hodgson

TITLE
Book Name: The Positive Behaviour Book
 75 Practical Strategies for Managing Classroom Behaviours
Book Number: S7
ISBN Number: 978-1-907269-39-4
UK Edition Published: 2010

AUTHOR
Patricia Hodgson

ACKNOWLEDGEMENTS
Designers: Mat Whittleston/Allie Browne
Illustrators: Akira Le Fevre/Allie Browne
Cover Design: Paul Sealey, PS3 Creative, 3 Wenworth Drive, Thornton, Lancashire
Printed in the UK for 'Topical Resources' by T.Snape and Co Ltd., Boltons Court, Preston, Lancashire.

UK PUBLISHER
Topical Resources
P.O. Box 329
Broughton
Preston
Lancashire
England
PR3 5LT

Tel: 01772 863158   Fax: 01772 866153

WEBSITE:
www.topical-resources.co.uk

E-MAIL:
sales@topical-resources.co.uk

COPYING NOTICE
This is a photocopiable book and permission is given to schools or teachers who buy this resource to make photocopies or transparencies of all pages. The copies must be for internal school use only, and may not be given or sold to other educational institutions or teachers from other institutions.

COPYRIGHT
Originally published in New Zealand © User Friendly Resources, 2006
UK Edition © Topical Resources, 2010.

Topical Resources specialises in publishing educational resources for teachers and pupils across a wide range of curriculum areas. If you wish to know more about our resources, or if you think your resource ideas have publishing potential, please visit our website or contact us using the information above.

Positive Behaviour — Contents

Introduction	4
Behaviour Specific Tips	7
Starting and Finishing	7-9
Time Issues	10
Individuals	14
Groups	28
Whole Class	31

Positive Behaviour — Introduction

When good classroom management systems are in place, teaching and learning can both occur more effectively. So my aim in developing this resource has been to provide classroom teachers and teaching assistants with practical and easy to implement ideas that will help classrooms to run more smoothly. All of the ideas in **The Positive Behaviour Book**, have been tried and tested by classroom teachers under the supervision of behaviour specialists.

The effectiveness of each of the strategies in this resource needs to be based on a consideration of the individual child's or class situation, their interests, and responsiveness to behavioural interventions. Not all approaches will work for all children and situations! You will also need to rely on your professional knowledge of the children and/or class group when selecting a strategy to implement.

It is my belief that pupils are more likely to interact responsibly when they are presented with choices, rather than having behaviour expectations imposed on them.

Happy teaching!

Patricia Hodgson

Positive Behaviour: Behaviour-Specific Tips

The Dreamer

For pupils who have difficulty following plans or who set unrealistic goals for themselves:

Work with the pupil to set and write down long-range goals. Break them into realistic, achievable steps or parts.

Use a guided questioning method with the pupil. For example, "What do you need, to do to get from here to there?"

Have the pupil set out a clear timetable that states when they will complete each step. This can also include what they need to do to achieve each step of their long-term goals. These pupils may need specific details, such as approximate times for achieving each step, included in their timetables. This is particularly important for assignment or project work.

Use guided questions to support the pupil's planning and monitor realistic aims. "How will you manage to do that?" Monitor the pupil's progress frequently with individual sessions.

The Flitter

For pupils who flit frequently from one activity to another, without completing any of them:

Be sure the pupil knows the complete requirements of the activity.

Highlight exactly what the completed activity will look like. For example, "When you have completed all six of the maths problems and have them corrected by me, you are finished. When you have finished you may go on to the creative design project."

Positive Behaviour — BEHAVIOUR-SPECIFIC TIPS

The Dawdler

For the pupil who has difficulty making transitions from one activity to another or one class to another:

Prepare the pupil for the transitions. Do this by providing advanced warnings of any change that will take place. The warning can include an expectation of behaviour and notice of what equipment they will need. The notice can be given in the following way, "We have one more worksheet to complete and then we will be going on to our structures projects. For this you will need your structures workbook and pencil. You can do that quickly and quietly, when we have finished this worksheet."

Write up the notice in point form on the board. This will reinforce the message.

Post a daily timetable in a visible spot outside the class or on the door, where pupils can see the structure of their day. Include approximate times and locations if relevant.

The Interrupter

For the pupil who constantly interrupts you with questions that are not related to work.

Set up a Question Box at the front of the room. Have the pupil post questions in there and let him/her know that you will get to them at break, lunchtime, or at the end of the day. Use a slip like the one below.

Name: _____   **Date:** _____

My question is: _____

_____

_____

Signed: _____

Positive Behaviour

STARTING AND FINISHING

1. New Pupil Welcome

Aim: To establish a supportive environment for new pupils who join your class (middle to upper primary - secondary) mid-way through the year

Materials: Brown paper bags, and items as per descriptors below

Strategy steps

a. All items are placed in the paper bag with the following note:

"The items in this bag have special meaning:
- The cotton wool is to remind you that this room is full of kind words and warm feelings.
- The chocolate is to comfort you if you are feeling sad.
- The tissue is to remind you to help dry someone else's tears.
- The sticker is to remind you that we all stick together and help each other.
- The star is to remind you to shine and always try your best.
- The gold thread is to remind you that friendship ties our hearts together.
- The coin is to remind you that you are valuable and special.
- The toothpick is to remind you to "pick out" the good qualities in your classmates.
- The rubber is to remind you that we all make mistakes, and that's OK.
- This letter is to remind you that you can always come and talk to me if you need.
- From your new teacher."

Before the pupil arrives, give the rest of the class a chance to look at this bag and discuss what they think about it.

2. Proactive Plans

Aim: To implement a low maintenance behaviour management method that fosters co-operative behaviours

Materials: None

Strategy steps

Begin each day with class discussions about class rules, expectations and possible class problems that may be encountered throughout the upcoming day.

The pupils may draw upon past experiences or current problems and concerns. This time may be used to develop social skill vocabulary through roleplays that focus on problem solving. Concepts such as respect, co-operation and responsibility may also be addressed. The class or individuals may work on concrete plans for solving particular problems.

Positive Behaviour

STARTING AND FINISHING

3. How's It Going?

Aim: To gain some insight into the emotional state of your pupils before the day begins

Materials: Pocket chart, lollipop sticks, paper circles, sticky tape

Strategy steps

Give each pupil a small paper circle and lollipop stick. Have them to draw a happy face on one side and a sad or angry face on the other side. They tape the faces to their lollipop stick. At the beginning of the day, pupils are to place their faces stick in the named pocket on the chart. They choose the face that they are most feeling like at that moment.

Sets of faces sticks may be created to extend the selection of faces available to pupils. This technique also provides an at-a-glance roll call for the teacher, to see who is present and who is away!

4. A Fun Finish

Aim: To reward positive whole class behaviours and end each day on a positive note

Materials: Depends on the game chosen

Strategy steps

Reserve the last 10-20 minutes of the class day for games.

The time spent on the games can be dependent upon the overall class behaviour for the day. This can be measured or be at your discretion. The main benefit of the fun finish is that pupils leave the classroom on a positive note, regardless of the minor altercations of the day. Leaving on such a note increases the possibility of a positive return!

Positive Behaviour

STARTING AND FINISHING

5. Sticky Specialist Lesson

Aim: To encourage positive behaviours across specialist classes: library, P.E., Art, Music

Materials: Stickers and sticker record card

Strategy steps

At the beginning of the year give each pupil a sticker record card. They must bring this to each class of the lesson it is for. Pupils hand in their card to you, or show their card on entry to the class.

Throughout the lesson, you can reward pupils with a sticker on their card. At the end of the year all pupils who have accumulated a set number of stickers are invited to attend a "special" party. Meeting the sticker quota is the only way to attend this party. Various specialist teachers may like to combine this technique to host a massive "special" party.

6. On Time Pass

Aim: To encourage frequently late pupils to be in class on time

Materials: Coloured reward slips

Strategy steps

This works best if it is used in a random manner. Before the bell, move around and talk to pupils who are either waiting appropriately outside the classroom or seated inside the room. This can be an excellent opportunity to informally chat with pupils.

After the bell, those pupils who were on time to class are rewarded with an on-time pass. This pass is worth two ticks on an On Time chart in the classroom. This is just a list of pupil names written on a marking grid and pinned up. At the end of the week or month, the ticks are totalled and some reward given for the punctual pupils.

The distribution of the passes must always remain a random, ever present possibility. After the first passes are distributed, outline the pass system with the class at the end of that lesson. Remind pupils that they must present their pass to get the ticks. Discretion is often needed, if this method is used within the first class of the day due to unforeseen lateness.

Positive Behaviour
TIME ISSUES

7. Trading Time

Aim: To record and reward positive behaviours

Materials: Stopwatch or timer

Strategy steps

When the class or target pupil is unruly or unsettled, hold up a timer to signify that the timer is on. Once the class or target pupil settles or is on-task, stop the timer and record the number of seconds.

At the end of the month or week, the total number of seconds recorded is tallied and subtracted from a set time of potential free choice activities. For example, if over a week the pupil clocked up five minutes of off-task time, this would be taken away from the potential total of 15 minutes. This pupil would then receive only 10 minutes of free choice time.

8. The Clock Is Ticking

Aim: To enable pupils to be accountable for their behaviour choices

Materials: Clock

Strategy steps

Tell the class group that whenever they are off task or wasting time, you will begin to time them and record the amount of time that is wasted.

During a suitable break, the time that has been wasted will be repaid in work time. Once the pupils are aware of this procedure you need to have some signal to show that you have begun timing.

Once pupils are aware that you are timing they fall very quickly into line. The key here is to always follow through with holding the group accountable for the time that is wasted. Peer pressure will work wonders in supporting this technique!

Positive Behaviour — TIME ISSUES

9. 1, 2, 3, 4 and 5!

Aim: To draw pupil attention quickly and quietly

Materials: Teacher's hand

Strategy steps

Tell pupils that when you require them to pay attention you will do the following:
Raise one hand above your head in a fist and slowly show all your fingers, until all five are visible.

By the time all five can be seen, the pupils should be watching and quiet. It may be suitable for the pupils to join with you in making the signal and you may like to count to five out loud, as you reveal your fingers.

10. Transition Time

Aim: To encourage pupils to be responsible for their behaviour choices and encourage quick and efficient class transitions

Materials: Blackboard / whiteboard

Strategy steps

The teacher informs the pupil group that the word TIME will be written on the top of the board. Each letter represents 15 seconds of stay-behind-time once it has been erased.

The letters can be erased by the teacher when the group is off task or unruly. At the end of the lesson, any time owed is repaid. This system works best when there is a whole school climate for being on-time to each and every lesson. If a class group accumulates too much time, too often, a school privilege may be removed.

Positive Behaviour — TIME ISSUES

11. My Time, Your Time

Aim: To maintain pupil attention during instruction

Materials: None

Strategy steps

Introduce the concept of "My Time" and "Your Time" to the group.

My Time is when the teacher teaches or gives instruction. During this time the group's job is to listen and not disturb another person.

Your Time is the last five minutes of the lesson or session, when the group may socially talk or have free time. Your Time is dependent upon the group's ability to act appropriately during My Time.

12. Wait Cards

Aim: To eliminate the pupil line up for work correction, and the behaviour problems that arise because of it

Materials: 10 small cards numbered 1 – 10 (one number per card). See page 60.

Strategy steps

The cards are kept in an accessible place near the teacher in order from 1-10. If the teacher is busy with another pupil, a card is taken from the front of the bundle, and the individual returns to their desk to go on with other work.

When the teacher is finished with the first pupil they call the missing number from the box, "One!" and that pupil is next to speak with the teacher. Their card is placed at the back of the bundle of numbers.

Ensure that the class has work to continue on with while waiting at their desk.

More cards could be made, but good management should keep the wait list to no more than 10 pupils.

Positive Behaviour — TIME ISSUES

13. Task Timer

Aim: To encourage time on task and completion of tasks

Materials: Kitchen timer or similar

Strategy steps

Each activity is set a specific time limit. Once the class group is clear on their job, the time limit is set and the timer started.

Pupils are encouraged to finish before the timer or by its "buzz".

14. Guided Choices

Aim: This method develops responsible choices without entering into the traditional power struggle. It is most suitable for pupils who often go head-to-head with authority

Materials: None

Strategy steps

The pupil is led to a desired activity through guided choices. If a pupil is required to line up and refuses, a guided choice may sound like this;

"John, it's time to line up. You can choose to line up at the front or at the end of the line."

The pupil does not view your instruction as a threat to their power, as they perceive that they are making the decision. This method is also very useful at home when trying to get a child to do something, "Do you want tidy your room before or after dinner?"

Positive Behaviour — INDIVIDUALS

15. Keeping Cheques

Aim: To develop responsibility for behaviours (with a twist of maths!)

Materials: Small bundles of papers stapled together as a cheque book. One per pupil

Strategy steps

Each pupil on the program receives a "cheque book" with a specific amount of money deposited in it, for example, £100.

Every time the pupil displays an inappropriate behaviour, they have to write a cheque for a previously agreed amount, such as, £10 for constant talking. They give you the cheque.

Any behaviour can be targeted with this program, from minor to major behaviour difficulties. Weekly or monthly rewards can be added for pupils with remaining money in their cheque books. This program also provides sneaky maths reinforcement as pupils keep check of their cheques!

16. Anger Jar

Aim: To allow pupils to get angry thoughts and feelings out of their systems by identifying what has made them angry and how they feel about it

Materials: Scrap paper and a jar with a lid

Strategy steps

The jar is placed on the teacher's desk or a prominent position. If a pupil feels angry about something or someone during the day, they write out their anger on a scrap piece of paper, fold it and place it in the jar.

At the end of the day the papers in the jar are destroyed and discarded. It is important that no questions are asked and that all papers remain confidential. The teacher can also use the jar to model how they handle angry thoughts and feelings.

Positive Behaviour — INDIVIDUALS

17. Blooming Success

Aim: To provide a tangible symbol of appropriate behaviours when success is observed

Materials: Drawing of flower and separate paper petals

Strategy steps

Draw the centre of a flower, and the flower's stem. Write the pupil's name in the centre of the flower. A pre-determined number of petals is gradually added to complete the flower. The number of petals must relate to the pupil's ability to be successful in reaching a desired behaviour goal. Each petal represents a behaviour achievement for a pre-selected target behaviour. For example, not calling out.

When the desired behaviour is observed, the pupil receives a petal to glue on to the flower drawing.

Once the flower is completed, an extra reward can be given. For example, a free choice activity can be offered or the completed flower can be displayed in a class garden.

18. Positive Behaviour Cards

Aim: To establish a consistent whole school approach to improving behaviour for individual pupils

Materials: Behaviour cards (see page 16)

Strategy steps

Positive behaviour cards are developed to suit the need and level of settings. For example, secondary cards include space to record behaviour for each class of that day; primary cards have space for each session or lesson.

The card is the responsibility of the pupil to carry for the day or days, as assigned, and present it to each class teacher at the end of the lesson or session. The class teacher comments on, or rates the pupil's behaviour for that lesson or session. At the end of the day the card is presented to the headteacher, Year level co-ordinator or class teacher.

The card is a formal, no-fuss means of closely monitoring pupil behaviours and can be set for use in both short and long time frames. The focus needs to be on pupils maintaining positive behaviours. Consequences need to be established for when pupil behaviour is below acceptable levels. For example, loss of break time rights for a card without any positive comments.

Always ensure consequences suit the individual pupil.

Positive Behaviour

INDIVIDUALS

POSITIVE BEHAVIOUR CARD

Name: _____
Date ___ / ___ / ___
Aim: _____

Session / Lesson	Comment	Initial
1. _____	_____	_____
2. _____	_____	_____
3. _____	_____	_____
4. _____	_____	_____
5. _____	_____	_____
6. _____	_____	_____
7. _____	_____	_____

Further comment

Signed _____

POSITIVE BEHAVIOUR CARD

Name: _____
Date ___ / ___ / ___
Aim: _____

Session / Lesson	Comment	Initial
1. _____	_____	_____
2. _____	_____	_____
3. _____	_____	_____
4. _____	_____	_____
5. _____	_____	_____
6. _____	_____	_____
7. _____	_____	_____

Further comment

Signed _____

Positive Behaviour — INDIVIDUALS

19. Fines and Bonus Points

Aim: To provide a means for building success for pupils with continual behavioural difficulties

Materials: None

Strategy steps

Decide on a target behaviour. Allocate 5 or 10 points to the pupil to begin with. Bonuses and fines are to be awarded for appropriate and inappropriate behaviours relating to the identified target.

Bonuses may include; following directions, telling the truth, politeness, self-control, responsibility, on task. Fines may include; not following directions, wasting time, rudeness, losing control, not telling the truth, not being responsible.

20. Chance Tickets

Aim: To encourage specific positive behaviours

Materials: Chance tickets

Strategy steps

Chance tickets can be used in a variety of ways. Pupils can be given a ticket for arriving to class on time, handing in homework or assignments on the day they are due or for other desired behaviours. See page 18.

The tickets can be collected by pupils, to redeem for a "chance". For example, 15 tickets can be redeemed for a homework chance, which allows the pupil to have an extra night to work on an assignment or task.

Positive Behaviour

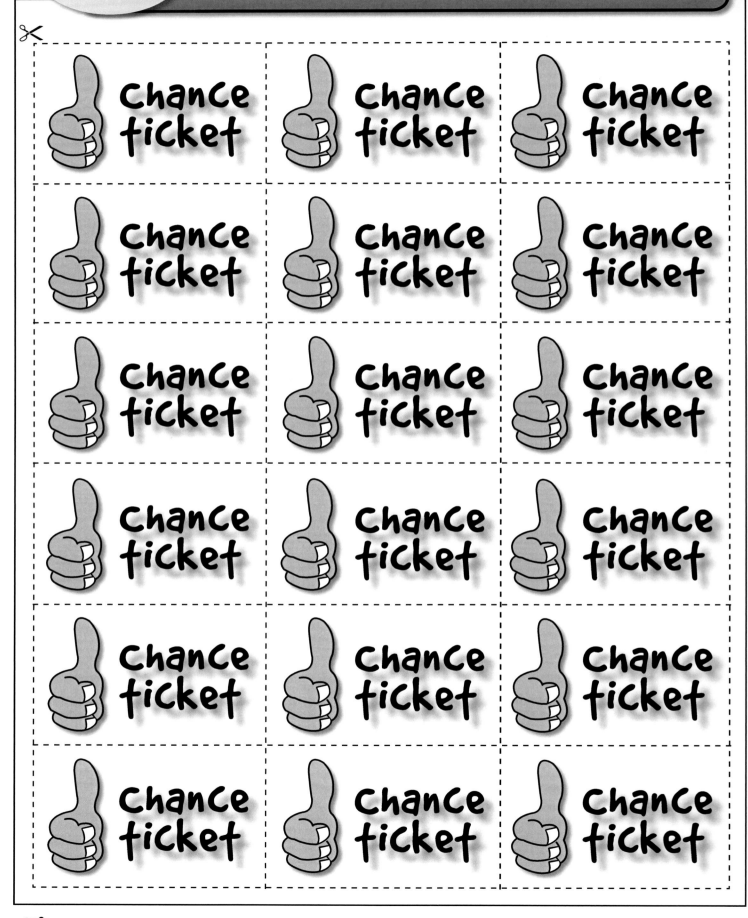

Positive Behaviour — INDIVIDUALS

21. Timely Tip!

Aim: To help slow starters get going

Materials: Egg timer or stopwatch

Strategy steps

Place the timer or watch in a place where the pupil can clearly see it. Decide on a time by which the pupil is to have started. For example, by the time the sand falls through once or by the two minute mark.

The timer can also be used to milestone the task. For example, "By four minutes I hope you are up to question three or by the time the timer is flipped twice…"

22. Feeling Faces

Aim: To allow pupils to express and identify their feelings

Materials: Quiet corner and face templates

Strategy steps

Set up an area where the pupils can go to calm down and have some quiet time. In this space set up the face templates (see pages 20-21).

In the quiet space the pupil uses a template to make a face that matches their feelings at that time. The face provides an excellent springboard for discussion about feelings and a means for identifying them.

The faces can also be used by other adults to discuss their feelings with the class or individual pupils.

Positive Behaviour

FEELING FACES

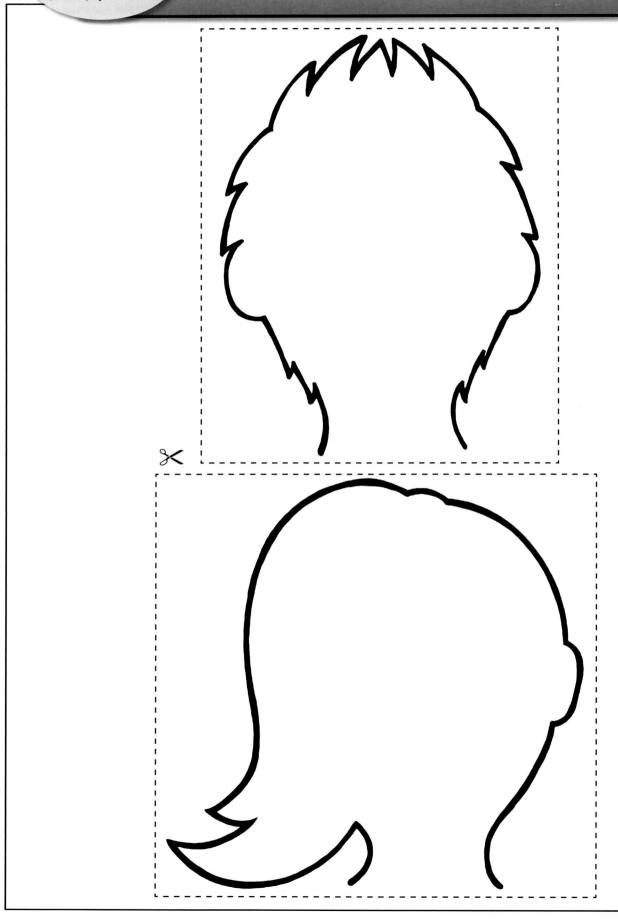

Positive Behaviour — FEELING FACES

Positive Behaviour — INDIVIDUALS

23. Punch Card

Aim: To record positive and desired behaviours

Materials: Fancy-shaped hole punch and punch cards

Strategy steps

Each pupil is given a card. When the pupil is observed doing the right thing, their card is given a hole punch by the teacher.

The holes can be used to buy things. For example, 30 holes entitles the pupil to a special treat, 25 holes may buy free choice of music during playtime in class, 10 holes may buy choice of seating for a day.

24. Signals

Aim: To provide a supportive environment for pupils having difficulty remaining on task, without lesson disruptions

Materials: None

Strategy steps

Signals can form a part of the behaviour management plan for the individual pupil with identified attention difficulties. These non-verbal signals can be developed in conjunction with the pupil to take the place of verbal reminders and prompts. The signal needs to be easily recognised by the pupil and easily implemented by the teacher. When the teacher notices the pupil is off-task or moving toward being off task, the signal can be given.

This strategy only works where the pupil accepts the difficulties they are having and is willing to make changes.

Positive Behaviour — INDIVIDUALS

25. Remind Me Cards

Aim: To enable self-regulation of inappropriate behaviours

Materials: Paper and contact

Strategy steps

With the pupil, identify the behaviour that is causing the most difficulty.

Have the pupil draw two pictures of this behaviour; one showing how it looks when they are engaged in this behaviour, and two, how it looks when they are doing the appropriate thing. Have these pictures stuck on to the pupil's desk along with a small grid of boxes. If the pupil is doing the right thing a tick is placed in the grid under the matching picture. The pupil's challenge is to achieve more ticks for the appropriate behaviours than for the other, or fill the grid of appropriate boxes first.

26. Time To Target?

Aim: To assist modification when pupils exhibit multiple inappropriate behaviours

Materials: None

Strategy steps

Identify and isolate the single behaviour that is causing the most stress. Make this and only this the focus of any intervention strategies. Focusing the pupil's attention on a single behaviour, for example, not calling out, heightens the opportunity for the pupil to experience success.

When the pupil is successful in one area, they often become successful in another as well.

Positive Behaviour — INDIVIDUALS

27. Keep In Touch Book

Aim: To maintain open communication links between home and school

Materials: A K.I.T. Book (an exercise book cut in half)

Strategy steps

The exercise book is sent between home and school daily. It is used for comments from both teachers and parents.

Where appropriate pupils can add their own comments.

28. Rule Role Models

Aim: To provide low key assistance to those pupils having behavioural difficulties

Materials: Class rules chart and photos or drawings of pupils

Strategy steps

Using an established class rules chart, choose a rule and place next to it a photo or drawing of the pupil who demonstrates the rule very well. This pupil may be someone who has already demonstrated the rule and is an excellent role model of how this rule is followed. Another approach to the rule models may be to rotate pupils across the class rules, where they have to focus on the particular rule they are matched to. Not forgetting the others of course!

If photos or drawings of pupils are difficult to access, the pupils could create a decorative version of their names, or design a symbol to represent themselves on the chart. It is important that this approach is implemented within a supportive environment, not one of identifying individual weaknesses.

Positive Behaviour

INDIVIDUALS

29. Menu For You

Aim: To develop some ownership for their behaviour from a target pupil.

Materials: A menu chart or card

Strategy steps

A menu of the types of rewards that would be suitable for the target behaviour achievements is developed in conjunction with the teacher and the pupil.

Depending on the age of the pupil, the menu can be a pictorial representation of the items or a written list. It may be decided that the pupil can only choose each item once, when goals are reached, or they may be ongoing.

30. Aggro 4 Av Time

Aim: To encourage positive behaviours from pupils who regularly use put downs or aggression

Materials: A selection of any or all of the following depending upon availability:
CD player, radio, TV and video, videos, DVDs, CDs, tapes, etc.
This method can be successfully implemented with only one AV selection

Strategy steps

Pupils with aggressive behaviours may earn AV time, where they can redeem points or time coupons in exchange for time listening to favourite CDs, radio, or watching a video.

Short cartoon segments on videotape are ideal to guide the amount of time spent and the nature of the content. Providing a menu or selection for pupils to choose from eliminates any inappropriate choices. CD choices may be limited to a certain number of songs, depending upon the points/time earned.

© UK Edition - Topical Resources. Copying permitted by purchasing schools only.

Positive Behaviour — INDIVIDUALS

31. A, B, C Certificates

Aim: To encourage specific targeted behaviours with immediate reinforcement

Materials: A, B, C Certificates (see pages 26, 27), box

Strategy steps

A certificate is given to the pupil for good behaviour. Depending on the type of behaviour the following certificate is given A = Academic, B = Behaviour, or C = Community.

Once the pupil has their certificate, they write their name on it and place it in a certificate box. At least once a week a name is drawn from the box. This pupil is allowed to choose from a selection of rewards. At the end of the week, all certificates are returned to the pupils to take home, and the process may begin again.

Remind pupils that the more certificates they earn, the more chances they have of being drawn from the box!

Congratulations!

To: _____

for excellent school work!

Awarded by: _____

Positive Behaviour — INDIVIDUALS

Congratulations!

To: _____

for excellent behaviour!

Awarded by: _____

Congratulations!

To: _____

for excellent caring!

Awarded by: _____

Positive Behaviour — GROUPS

32. The Ticket Program 1

Aim: To improve the behaviours of individuals and small groups

Materials: Raffle tickets or small papers as tickets

Strategy steps

A group or a pupil who wants to change a negative behaviour, identifies what that behaviour is.

At the start of the day the pupil or group receives 3 tickets. Each time anyone displays the behaviour they wish to change, the pupil must give the teacher one ticket.

If a pupil or group loses all of their tickets, 5 minutes are deducted from their play, each time the negative behaviour is seen. At the end of the day, pupils with tickets gain a star or a stamp. Pupils who reach a predetermined total may gain extra time in a chosen activity. Another option is for the tickets to go into a barrel for a monthly/weekly prize. Pupils can also earn back their lost tickets if positive behaviours are observed.

Caution: This programme may not suit all pupils. Pupils with severe behaviour difficulties may not respond.

33. Marbles in the Jar

Aim: To develop appropriate group behaviours

Materials: Marbles and a large preserving jar

Strategy steps

This system is easy to establish and maintain. Each working group in the class is allocated a different coloured marble. Groups try to fill a jar with marbles of their own colour. Marbles are added to the jar when groups are on task or demonstrate particularly good behaviour. When the agreed amount of marbles is reached, at the end of the week, or if the jar is full, a count is done and the winning group receives a reward that has been agreed upon. If a pupil in a group is behaving inappropriately you can give marbles to the rest of the groups. The social pressure that the pupil will receive from other group members quickly pulls the person into line.

Positive Behaviour / GROUPS

34. Popcorn Praise

Aim: To focus on the positives in the entire class

Materials: Popcorn kernels and containers

Strategy steps:

This can be used over a complete week.
Each time a pupil is praised the teacher gives them any number of kernels.

Praise can be given for any reason. For example, "I like having you in my class. Here's 10 kernels!" The children can also use the kernels to reward each other throughout the week. At the end of the week, the pupils get to cook and eat their popcorn.

Some pupils may choose to pool their kernels and this is fine, as it encourages co-operation and sharing! This also gives some idea of how much praise you use in your classroom.

35. Group Gardens

Aim: To encourage group co-operation to attain long-term goals through specific behaviours

Materials: Drawing of flower and separate paper petals

Strategy steps

This follows the form of Blooming Success (pg 15), but at a group level. The group is set a target behaviour to work towards. Each time the behaviour is displayed by any member of the group, a petal is placed on the group's flower.

When the group's flower is complete it is placed in a window box. Each group has their own window box to fill with flowers. Once the window box is full, the group may be given a reward. This can also be used with the whole class, if the target behaviours suit a whole class approach.

Positive Behaviour — GROUPS

36. Tally Ho!

Aim: To encourage co-operation and positive behaviours within small groups

Materials: None

Strategy steps

Each small group decides on a name for themselves. This name is placed on the board, in a place where it can remain for the day or week.

Each time positive or desired behaviours are seen, the group is awarded tally marks on the board. Tally marks can also be lost, due to poor behaviour. The group with the most points at the end of the week gains a small treat.

37. Tally Tubs

Aim: To provide a tangible means for rewarding appropriate behaviours

Materials: Boxes and tokens

Strategy steps

Divide the class into groups and provide each group with a box. The group may decorate the box to make it easily identified as theirs.

The tokens are kept by the teacher and placed in the box when appropriate behaviours are seen. At the end of the designated time, week or day, the group with the highest number of tokens is the winner.

The behaviour boxes can also be used to target specific behaviours for each individual group.

Positive Behaviour

WHOLE CLASS

38. Great Groups

Aim: To maintain noise control of group work activities without disrupting the entire class.

Materials: Coloured circles – green, red, yellow, one set per group

Strategy steps

Prepare one set of coloured cardboard circles for each group – red, green, yellow. It may be best to laminate them for long term use.

If a group is working well and using quiet voices they are given a green circle. This circle means **excellent job**.

If a group is getting a bit loud, they are given a yellow circle which means **warning – you need to quiet down.**

If a group is very loud and noisy they are given a red circle. This circle can mean **quiet now or see me at lunch.**

Each of the circles needs to be introduced to the class group before they are used. This is a wonderful time saver, as you don't need to interrupt the entire class to get one group back on track!

39. Likes and Dislikes Sheets

Aim: To identify pupil interest areas, likes and dislikes

Materials: Likes and Dislikes Sheets or drawing paper and colours (see page 32)

Strategy steps

This is best used in the first few weeks of school, or when a teacher is new to a class group. The pupils are invited to complete a sheet of likes and dislikes, favourite class and school activities, favourite home activities, etc. This information can be kept on file for teacher reference in the set up of individual behaviour management plans that effectively tap into pupil motivations.

Each pupil is given a large sheet of drawing paper, to divide into the various areas in question. Pupils may then draw out their likes and dislikes, perhaps with some words to describe what is taking place in each representation.

Positive Behaviour

WHOLE CLASS

Name: _____

More about me...

The **best thing** I've ever done is _____

I'd like to **visit** _____

My **favourite food** is _____

My **favourite work** at school is _____

During **breaktime** I really like to _____

When I am at **home** I like to _____

My favourite **animal** is _____

My **best friend's** name is _____

I really **like** it when _____

My favourite **TV show** is _____

If I could be any **famous person** I'd like to be _____

My **favourite place** to be is _____

My **favourite colour** is _____

My favourite thing to do in my **free time** is _____

When I **feel happy** I like to _____

If I am **feeling angry** I like to _____

My **favourite job** in the class is _____

I really like to **sit near** _____

I'm pretty **good at** _____

I need **some help** with _____

Positive Behaviour — WHOLE CLASS

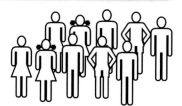

40. Coin Days

Aim: To encourage appropriate behaviours within a long-term management approach, utilising maths and money skills

Materials: Two non-see-through jars, plastic coins, money box-type storage for each pupil, plastic counters with either 5 or 10 written on them, marker pens

Strategy steps

At the end of each day pupils chosen for displaying good behaviours, receive a dip from the jar for one coin. (Remember the jar contains a variety of fake coins of differing value.) The coins retrieved remain with the pupil in their individual money box.

As the pupils collect their coins, they may trade up for larger coins, e.g. 2 x 5p coins may be exchanged for 1 x 10p coin, or similar amounts for a £1 or £2 coin. When the pupil has achieved the set target amount, e.g. £5, they may trade all their coins for a reward.

Rewards may include 20 minutes free time, a sweet treat, sit by a friend for the day, sit at the teacher's desk for the day, etc.

If the class has a day where every pupil receives a dip in the jar, a plastic counter is drawn from another jar, with either five or 10 points on it. These points are class points, which are tallied separately from the coin amounts. The class points also have a target, perhaps 200. When the class has reached the class target, a class party may be held. Throughout the year the class may reach target as many times as they can. Different ideas for class parties include, ice cream party, popcorn party, video party, games party, theme party.

Extra dips may be given for helpers, being kind, responsible behaviours, quality work, excellent team work. The sky's the limit! This approach also provides a great boost for teaching units on money!

Positive Behaviour — WHOLE CLASS

41. Ponder Progress

Aim: To provide a record of behaviours that focuses on self worth and value

Materials: Exercise book

Strategy steps

From the beginning of the school year, the teacher records the strategies that are implemented for particular challenging behaviours.

This record notes the types of behaviours and also any improvements. Over the course of each term, the record book is completed and then reviewed. This book provides an excellent means for seeing the full picture of behaviour management plans that were implemented throughout the year. Often these strategies are not remembered in the day to day routine of school. This book is also a helpful resource for report writing times and parent interviews!

42. Ignoring Game

Aim: To allow pupils to practise ignoring skills to remain on-task in real life situations

Materials: None

Strategy steps

The pupils are taught the individual steps in ignoring unwanted attention. For example, making no eye contact, no smiling, no talking, turning away from the distractor, imagining the other person is invisible.

Small roleplays can be set up, either with the whole class or on an individual basis, where a pupil attempts to distract the others and gain their attention. The goal of this activity is for the other pupils to ignore these attempts to distract them. The distractor may attempt to distract by talking, taking their things, smiling, touching and through other typical classroom behaviours.

The pupils who ignore properly, may have a turn at being the distractor. This ignoring behaviour may be included on the collection of class reward points.

Positive Behaviour — WHOLE CLASS

43. Word Watch!

Aim: To reward the class for good behaviour on a weekly basis

Materials: Chalkboard or whiteboard and chalk/pen

Strategy steps

Choose a word of at least six letters to be the "word to watch".

Write the word on the board using large letters in an easy-to-see spot.

Explain to the class that they will get a reward if they can keep at least one of these letters on the board by the end of the week. They gain and lose letters for their behaviours. This method can be used very effectively to monitor lining up, entering leaving class and for bringing a class to attention. If the class becomes too noisy or off task, the teacher without speaking, goes to the board and erases a letter. It's amazing how quickly this settles the group!

If by Friday, the class still has at least one letter in the word to watch, they gain a class reward. Suitable rewards include; extra points on star charts, a class video, extra time in a chosen activity, or if appropriate, extra playtime.

44. Mystery Person

Aim: To develop appropriate whole class behaviours

Materials: None

Strategy steps

Place all of the pupils' names in a box and draw one name out. DO NOT tell the class who it is. Put the name in a place out of reach. This pupil becomes the mystery person for the day.

If the mystery person has a good behaviour day, then that person can choose a game for the whole class to play for the last 10 or 20 minutes. Throughout the day the class are to be reminded of the mystery person and of the type of behaviour that is expected from them all. A class menu of games and activities for the mystery pupil to choose from can also be established.

© UK Edition - Topical Resources. Copying permitted by purchasing schools only.

Positive Behaviour — WHOLE CLASS

45. Let's Have A Laugh!

Aim: To diffuse tension in the room, show pupils how to respond to teasing, and build resilience.

Materials: A large cardboard box, felt pens, coloured paper, glue, scissors

Strategy steps:

This tip gives you an opportunity to talk with pupils about the difference between laughing together and laughing at someone. Sometimes pupils need help to recognise the difference and know how to react to it.

As a class build a "laughing box". Everyone contributes to making the box, and everyone has their name on it, including the class teacher. The box is decorated to be bright and cheerful. Each pupil creates a name plaque decorated in their own special way and pastes it onto the box.

Some people may bring funny photos of themselves or family members to put in the box. Others may bring special items that are attached to a funny situation about themselves. The class may write down things that have happened that have been funny or brought a lot of joy to the group. Keep adding to the box all the time.

When the time seems right pull items out of the box and share and laugh together. Pupils can also do this in small groups. The box should be on display all the time so new things can be added and so that items can be shared when laughing is needed.

46. Noise Dial

Aim: To encourage self-regulation of classroom noise levels

Materials: Noise dial (see page 37)

Strategy steps

The noise dial can be drawn on a side section of the blackboard or constructed out of card. The dial has increments of noise types like silence, whisper, group talking, games noise.

The dial is set to the most suitable noise level for each class activity or altered as noise levels need adjusting. If the dial is drawn on the board, the arrow will need to be re-drawn as the noise changes. If the dial is constructed, a paper clip needs to be used so that the arrow is able to be moved, as needed.

Once the class are used to the settings, they can be encouraged to determine the appropriate noise levels for an activity.

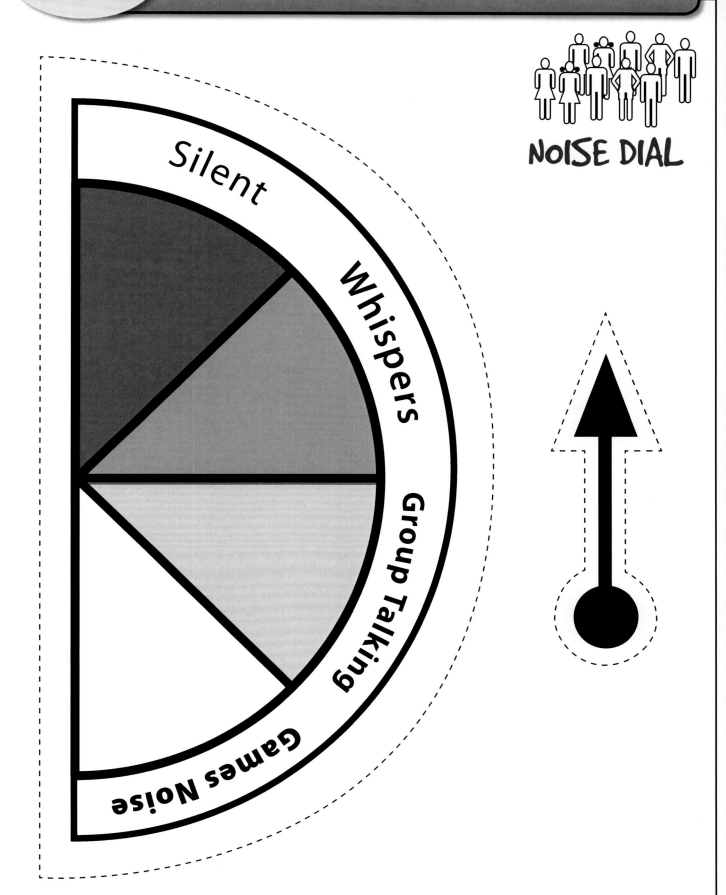

Positive Behaviour

WHOLE CLASS

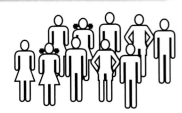

47. Race Around the Class

Aim: To encourage appropriate whole class behaviours

Materials: Board game type track and cardboard cars

Strategy steps

Give each pupil a cardboard car, which they can decorate.

The cars are placed on the starting space of the board. Each time a positive behaviour is noted or a reward is given the pupil may be granted "so-many" spaces to move their car.

The cars can be attached to the board with blue-tac, so they are easily removed as needed. If a pupil completes the course they may gain extra time rewards, etc. Once the entire class has completed the board, a whole class reward may be granted, such as class party, special choice video, pop corn party, BBQ, etc.

48. The Silence Game

Aim: To encourage group silence without individual rewards

Materials: Stopwatch

Strategy steps

This game can be played whenever you need the class to settle and be quiet. It is utilised in the same manner as your call for quiet, but this time it is made into a game.

The Silence Game begins with the class getting three seconds to make noise, then on the teacher's signal they are to be silent for as long as possible. This effort is timed, with the challenge being to see how long they can remain quiet. Past class efforts may be hailed as the ones to beat in the initial stages of the game, and then their current times become their goals. This technique allows success to be its own reward!

Positive Behaviour — WHOLE CLASS

49. Ring! Ring!

Aim: To encourage attention to appropriate behaviours at all times

Materials: A bell

Strategy steps

Ring a bell at any time during the day.

Points or a reward to those individuals who are on task or sitting at their seats, or displaying a targeted behaviour.

50. Cheers and Tears

Aim: To provide an outlet for pupils to express their feelings

Materials: Two medium-sized boxes, decorated – one for tears and one for cheers

Strategy steps

The pupils write down their messages to the teacher and place them in either of the two boxes. Tears for sad messages and cheers for happy messages (see pg 40). The teacher privately reads the messages as appropriate and responds to the pupils in written form.

Often pupils will express themselves more openly when there is some distance between themselves and the teacher. It also provides a cooling off time when things become heated.

Positive Behaviour

😊 Happy Message

Dear _____

_____
_____
_____ **Signed** _____

😊 Happy Message

Dear _____

_____
_____
_____ **Signed** _____

☹ Sad Message

Dear _____

_____
_____
_____ **Signed** _____

☹ Sad Message

Dear _____

_____
_____
_____ **Signed** _____

Positive Behaviour — WHOLE CLASS

51. The Positive Drawing

Aim: To encourage positive behaviours

Materials: Paper slips and a box or jar

Strategy steps

When pupils are identified as behaving positively, they are allowed to write their name on a slip of paper and put it in the box/jar.

At the end of a designated time, maybe the month or the week, the teacher behaviours the positive drawing, where a name is drawn from the jar/box. This pupil may receive a special reward.

52. Class Compliment Chain

Aim: To develop a class goal based upon appropriate behaviours

Materials: Paper clips and a notice board

Strategy steps

The class discusses what compliments are, and how they may sound in everyday life. Write down a shared list. For example, "I really like your...."

As a group their goal is to get compliments, from others within or outside of the school, if on excursions, for appropriate behaviours. Each compliment gains them a paper clip which is joined to the last. The paper clips are placed on the notice board, where their mission is to reach a set point on the board. Once the target is reached a class party or class reward may be given.

Positive Behaviour — WHOLE CLASS

53. Coaching Comments

Aim: To provide verbal and written encouragement to pupils in a variety of ways

Materials: None

Strategy steps

Each comment can be given to pupils individually or as a whole class.

- Nobody does it better!
- Now you have it!
- Nothing can stop you!
- Great job!
- This made my day!
- Marvellous work!
- You've mastered this!
- You're unreal!
- What a master!
- Great improvement!
- This is really great!
- Tremendous!
- That's awesome!
- Fantastic!
- That's incredible!
- You make it look easy!
- Keep it up!
- This is better than ever!
- Excellent effort!
- That's sensational!
- Congratulations!
- Outstanding effort!
- Perfect in every way!
- You can be proud of yourself!
- Wonderful job!
- Good thinking!
- Cool!
- Super!
- You're doing much better!
- Keep up the good work!
- You're learning so well!
- That's the way!
- This is the best ever!
- You make teaching fun!
- That's it!
- Great going!
- Too easy!
- Good for you!
- Fine effort!
- U R Gr8
- You're unbelievable!
- That's just super!
- Couldn't be better!
- Beautiful to behold!
- Incredible effort!
- Your personal best!
- What an achievement!
- World-class effort!
- Dynamite work!
- It's great working with you!
- This is first class!
- Now you've got the hang of it!
- You are very good at this!

Positive Behaviour — WHOLE CLASS

54. Musical Moments

Aim: To provide non-verbal messages for gaining pupil attention

Materials: An inexpensive wind-up music box

Strategy steps

Wind-up the music box fully every morning before the class arrives.

Tell your class that each time they are too noisy or off task, the music box will be opened and the music will play until they get back on task or quiet down. If at the end of the day there is any music left in the box, the class will receive some reward. This reward may take the form of points collected for use at the end of the week free choice time. The key here is to find a reward that truly motivates the class.

55. Colour Cards

Aim: To encourage positive behaviours

Materials: Named class pocket chart or individual pupil letterboxes, coloured cards - index card sized (red, green and yellow)

Strategy steps

Pupils are informed that they may receive one of the coloured cards during the day.

Each card has a different meaning:
Red: There will be a consequence! (decided on and explained earlier)
Yellow: Warning; watch out!
Green: You're doing well!

Positive Behaviour — WHOLE CLASS

56. Positive Lollipops

Aim: To encourage positive behaviours

Materials: Lollipop sticks and felt pens

Strategy steps

Using coloured felt pens write a number of different encouraging statements on each of the lollipop sticks, for example **Super Effort** or **Great Helper.**

When pupils receive a certain number of sticks they may gain a reward.

57. Class Reflection

Aim: To encourage whole class reflection their behaviours.

Materials: Behaviour chart

Strategy steps

As a whole class identify behaviours that are positive and list them on the behaviour chart. This chart needs to be displayed in a prominent place, where pupils can easily view it throughout the day.

At the end of each day use the chart to talk about the behaviours that have been shown. Individual pupils may be recognised for their great behaviour, or behaviours not achieved may become a focal point for the following day.

Positive Behaviour — WHOLE CLASS

58. Surprise Can

Aim: To reinforce positive pupil behaviours

Materials: Large coffee can, lollipop sticks, felt pens, paint or dytex dyes

Strategy steps

Decorate the coffee can brightly and paint or dye the sticks different colours. Once dry, label each stick with a different reward or special job.

Place the sticks in the coffee can. The teacher draws out a stick for individuals or groups of pupils who have finished their work, set great examples, etc. These pupils get to undertake the reward on the stick. Pupils may also be allowed to draw out a surprise stick. It may be helpful to use a record chart to keep track of which pupils are using the surprise can.

59. Behaviour Certificates

Aim: To encourage consistent, good behaviour choices between class teachers and specialist teachers: (music, art, supply teachers etc)

Materials: Behaviour certificates (see page 46) and items for a Treasure Box Dip

Strategy steps

Tell the class group that the specialist teacher or supply teacher will have "Awesome Behaviour Certificates" to give out during their day or lesson.

These certificates, given out very sparingly, entitle the bearer to take a dip from the treasure box. Items suitable for the box included pencils, erasers, notebooks. The awesome behaviour certificates can be placed on the teacher's desk in a secure spot or given out to the specialist teachers to use with your class.

Positive Behaviour — WHOLE CLASS

AWESOME BEHAVIOUR!
You were great today!

Presented to: _____
Class: _____

AWESOME BEHAVIOUR!
You were a pleasure to have in the class today!

Presented to: _____
Class: _____

AWESOME BEHAVIOUR!
You were a top pupil today!

Presented to: _____
Class: _____

Positive Behaviour — WHOLE CLASS

60. Mini-Oscar Achievers

Aim: To reinforce class rules in a novel manner

Materials: Record chart, novel pens, pencils, rubbers, certificates (see page 48)

Strategy steps

This technique is best suited to younger children. All pupil names are placed on the record chart. This chart needs to allow for at least 25-30 tick spaces alongside each pupil.

Once the class rules have been established, pupils are told that each time they are observed keeping a class rule, their named will be ticked. Their aim is to fill all the spaces with ticks. The first pupil to achieve this, is named the first place achiever, and the next three highest achievers are also recognised. Once the goal has been met, a mini-awards ceremony is held. You may like to make a class event of it, by inviting the parents and headteacher to attend.

The achievers are presented with a certificate, and pens, pencils and rubbers, or similar. The ceremony includes photo sessions to record the moment! This technique may be repeated at a later stage of the year.

61. Listen In

Aim: To provide targets for the whole class to work towards

Materials: Radio or CD player

Strategy steps

Pupils collectively choose a target behaviour to work on. If they are able to be successful at this behaviour, they earn the right to listen to their choice of radio or CD during the next art time or free activity time.

Positive Behaviour

THREE LEVELS OF ACHIEVEMENT

Mini-oscar Achiever Award

And the **Mini-oscar Achiever Award** goes to...

_____

for **Outstanding Achievement** in...

_____

Highest Achiever Award

And the **Highest Achiever Award** goes to...

_____

for **Fantastic Achievement** in...

_____

Achiever Award

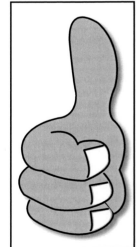

And the **Achiever Award** goes to...

_____

for **Achievement** in...

_____

Positive Behaviour

WHOLE CLASS

62. Stars and Squares

Aim: To motivate the entire class to work together for great classroom behaviour

Materials: A blank hundred square counting chart, star stickers, dot stickers

Strategy steps

Using an empty counting chart, place a few randomly spread stars in some squares. When pupils show positive behaviours, a dot is placed in the first square.

This continues for other behaviours as the board is slowly filled. Once the class reaches a star they may choose a class reward. The final celebration takes place on completion of the chart. This may be a class party or similar group reward.

63. Point Taken!

Aim: To establish a simple no-fuss management plan for the whole class

Materials: Points chart

Strategy steps:

All pupil names are placed on the points chart. This chart has space for the names and space for tally marks or points. The goal here is for the pupils to avoid achieving five points. Any behaviour that disrupts learning and teaching earns a point. The interaction is should be no-fuss and simple, "J. that's one point on the chart."

More serious disruptions such as injuring another pupil may warrant a flat five point penalty. At the end of the week pupils with fewer than five points receive a reward. This technique may also be implemented by giving all pupils five points, at the beginning of the week, and their goal is to keep some points by the end of the week.

Positive Behaviour — WHOLE CLASS

64. Reach for the Stars!

Aim: To encourage positive helping behaviours

Materials: Pocket chart, cut-out shapes, stars, brown buttons

Strategy steps

Each pupil receives a pocket on the chart with their name on it. Pupils are rewarded with a star in their pocket for helping and co-operative behaviours.

If they display negative behaviours they receive a brown button in their pocket. They cannot have both stars and buttons in the pocket at the same time. All stars are lost, if a button is gained, but pupils may have more than one star in their pocket. It is also possible to lose a star, instead of gaining a button.

This depends upon the nature of the behaviours. Each week the number of stars are counted. This may result in a reward, or you may monitor pupil star progress with a chart record and review this at the end of each month.

65. Auction Action

Aim: To provide reinforcement of positive behaviours

Materials: Positive pounds (page 51), inexpensive prize collection

Strategy steps

Pupils earn points for positive behaviours throughout the week.
At the end of the week or month, one point earns one positive pound.

Pupils can use the money earned to bid on different prizes from the prize collection. A mini-auction is conducted by the class teacher. If using Monopoly money instead, be sure to mark the school ones with a personal mark of yours, to ensure pupils don't bring in extra "cash" from home! This technique provides an excellent chance to reinforce maths and social skills.

Positive Behaviour

AUCTION POUNDS

1 POSITIVE POUND	1 POSITIVE POUND
1 POSITIVE POUND	1 POSITIVE POUND
1 POSITIVE POUND	1 POSITIVE POUND
1 POSITIVE POUND	1 POSITIVE POUND
1 POSITIVE POUND	1 POSITIVE POUND

Positive Behaviour

WHOLE CLASS

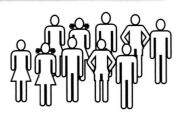

66. Jelly Good!

Aim: To provide a fair positive reward system, not just based on being the "best" behaved

Materials: Large clear jar or container, jelly beans, record book

Strategy steps

Pupils are rewarded for positive behaviours or doing their best, making an effort, being helpful, etc., with the chance to guess the number of jelly beans in the jar.

The guesses can be recorded over the week or a month, and then the closest guess to the actual number, gets to keep the beans. In the event of a tie, the beans are split between the guessers. The guesses are recorded in the guess book, which records name, date, guess.

The number of beans does not need to completely fill the jar, sometimes it may be a smaller number of beans to guess. This can also be implemented with other heat resistant sweets—soft lollies, crisps (this is really tricky!), twisties … the options are endless! Enjoy!

67. Make Their Day!

Aim: To encourage positive classroom behaviours

Materials: None

Strategy steps

Pupils make their day by earning a set number of points for positive behaviours. This earns them one day.

Their target is ten days, where they receive a very small reward and move to the next level. This level may have an increased target and increased rewards.

Positive Behaviour — WHOLE CLASS

68. Kind Acts and Good Deeds

Aim: To encourage and foster acts of kindness and good deeds

Materials: 10–15 small cards per pupil (see pg 54), a jar

Strategy steps

Each pupil is given a set of cards to keep at their desk. Whenever they do a kind deed or respond positively to a negative situation, they may place their name on a card and place it in the jar.

The pupil must first explain to the teacher what the situation was and how they acted. Each Friday three to five names may be drawn from the jar for special recognition and sharing of what they did and how they did it. This is an excellent social skills teaching opportunity!

69. Trade In

Aim: To encourage positive behaviours while fostering responsibility

Materials: Stamps or stickers, record card, reward choices

Strategy steps

Each pupil receives a record card, on which they place the stamps or stickers they earn for positive behaviours.

After five stamps or stickers are received, they may trade in their card for a treat from the reward choices. If a pupil breaks a rule they receive an X on their card. Two X's and the parents are contacted, three X's and they earn a detention. The good news is that three stamps or stickers can remove an X.

Positive Behaviour

KIND ACTS & GOOD DEEDS

I did a good deed today	I did a good deed today
name: _____	name: _____
date: _____	date: _____

I did a good deed today	I did a good deed today
name: _____	name: _____
date: _____	date: _____

I did a kind act today	I did a kind act today
name: _____	name: _____
date: _____	date: _____

I did a kind act today	I responded positively to a negative situation today
name: _____	name: _____
date: _____	date: _____

I responded positively to a negative situation today	I responded positively to a negative situation today
name: _____	name: _____
date: _____	date: _____

© UK Edition - Topical Resources. Copying permitted by purchasing schools only.

Positive Behaviour — WHOLE CLASS

70. Lights Out!

Aim: To implement a non-verbal management strategy that gains pupil attention

Materials: None

Strategy steps

When the class group becomes noisy and unruly, switch off the classroom lights. The sudden darkness from the lights being turned off captures the group's attention instantly.

From here it is easy to give instruction or bring correction, without having to raise your voice above the din!

Do not over use this technique or it will lose its effectiveness!

71. Get Your Thinking Hat On!

Aim: To get pupils to collectively think about how to manage negative behaviours in the class

Materials: Thinking Hats template (page 56)

Strategy steps

Using the Edward De Bono's Thinking Hats strategy is an excellent way to discuss negative behaviours in the class. Each thinking hat directs a different way of thinking. Pose the question "What Can We Do To Improve Behaviour in Our Class?" and then apply the hats strategy.

THE WHITE HAT is used to gather all the facts, the things we know to be true, information and data.
THE RED HAT is used to separate our emotions from the facts; it is how we feel about something or how it makes us feel.
THE BLACK HAT is our critical judgement; the negative aspects or the bad things attached to the topic.
THE GREEN HAT this represents unlimited thinking, new ideas, possibilities, almost the extreme of our ideas, ideas that are "right out there."
THE BLUE HAT is the controlling or calming hat that brings our thinking back into line, implements new ideas
THE YELLOW HAT is the positive aspect of an idea or topic or issue, all the good things about something.

Positive Behaviour

THINKING HATS TEMPLATE

White Hat

Red Hat

Black Hat

Green Hat

What can we do to improve the behaviour in our class?

Blue Hat

Yellow Hat

Positive Behaviour — WHOLE CLASS

72. Tell Mr. Tattle

Aim: To eradicate constant tale telling.

Materials: A box or container decorated with a sad face, scrap paper

Strategy steps

Have a class discussion about telling tales. Tell the class that if they have a tale that must be told, they are to write or draw it on a piece of paper and place it in Mr. Tattle.

The teacher and Mr. Tattle will discuss all the tales after school each day… If there are any at all after this system is set up!

Assure the class that any tales that need your assistance will be dealt with.

Make certain that the class understands the difference between those urgent issues and those that can wait!

73. Card Count

Aim: To monitor positive behaviours across the group setting.

Materials: Pupil pocket chart, three coloured cards per pupil – red, green, yellow

Strategy steps:

Each pupil receives one of each coloured cards in their pocket. The cards are placed in order: green, yellow, red, with green at the front. If throughout the day a pupil breaks a class rule, the green card is taken from their pocket to reveal the yellow card. This means they have five minutes in the time out space or similar action.

When they have returned to their desk with appropriate behaviours, the green card is replaced. The red card is displayed for more serious disruptive or disobedient behaviours. The red card may signal the pupil is to go to the office or a parallel class for 10 minutes, or similar action. Ensure that the pocket chart is visible to all pupils.

Have the actions clearly established before implementing the technique.

Positive Behaviour — WHOLE CLASS

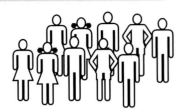

74. Setting A Positive Classroom Tone

Classroom tone, set by the teacher, makes a huge difference to the way pupils behave towards each other. If teachers can address pupils positively, smile, and encourage feelings of worth and connectedness, pupils will follow this behaviour in their peer relationships.

- Provide a mirror in the classroom with a sign attached to the reflective side which says "Hello, I like you!" Change the sign from time to time with "This smile belongs to you," or "Hello, you look like a real winner today!" and so on.

- Find a bright, colourful jacket that you can hang on your chair. Tell pupils that any time they want some TLC, want to tell you something, need someone to talk to, or want some quiet time, they can wear the jacket. This gives you a cue to follow up on an issue with the pupil. It also helps pupils to report something by breaking the ice through wearing the jacket first.

- To teach about no put-downs use a large doll. The teacher can use the doll to show the full range of put-downs form verbal to non-verbal, including face-pulling, eye-rolling, arm folding, back turning etc.. Using the doll means that a pupil is not inadvertently set up as a target.

Positive Behaviour — WHOLE CLASS

75. Reward Ideas!

- Sit at the teacher's desk
- Take care of class pets for the day/night
- Have lunch with your favourite school person
- Have afternoon tea with the headteacher
- Teacher phones the pupil's parents to tell them how great they have been
- Draw on the whiteboard/blackboard
- Be first in line
- Do only half an assignment
- Choose any class job for the week
- Choose the music for art time
- Do all the class jobs for a day
- Invite a visitor to spend a day at school
- Get a drink whenever you want
- Use the pencil sharpener whenever you like
- No early morning work
- No homework
- Be a class helper for another room
- Help the school secretary
- Help the headteacher
- Help the librarian
- Stay in the class and play board games with a friend at lunch
- Use the good work stamps
- Use the teacher's chair
- Take a class game home for the night
- Choose a book for the teacher to read to the class
- Move your desk for a day
- Keep a toy on your desk for a day
- Lunch with the teacher
- Use the beanbag for the day
- Use the computer
- Be the first to eat lunch

Positive Behaviour — WAIT CARDS

WAIT CARD **1.**	WAIT CARD **6.**
WAIT CARD **2.**	WAIT CARD **7.**
WAIT CARD **3.**	WAIT CARD **8.**
WAIT CARD **4.**	WAIT CARD **9.**
WAIT CARD **5.**	WAIT CARD **10.**